Get on the 7 Streams Team

*How to Discover Your Multiple
Streams of Income*

Tip Jones

Ganny Pie Media & Publishing
info@gannypie.com
www.gannypie.com

Ordering Information:

Quantity sales. Special discounts are available on quantity purchases by corporations, associations, trade bookstores, wholesalers and others. For details, contact the publisher at the address above.

Printed in the United States of America
First Printing, 2015
ISBN-13: 978-1519273321

Free Access to Module 1 of the GET ON THE 7 STREAMS TEAM Online Coaching Program

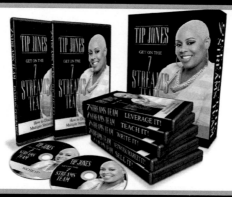

TABLE OF CONTENTS

INTRO

The Beauty of ~~Simplicity~~ Multiplicity

I have yet to meet someone who does not desire both wealth and ample time to enjoy it. Who really wants to wait until age 65 to do what they love?—to travel and spend their hard-earned money? The truth is, many will indeed wait but do not have to.

Too many of us smart, innovative, inventive, entrepreneurial individuals are working for someone else 160 hours a month while trying to effectively build pioneering enterprises and sticking their hands into a salad bowl of prospective business ideas. By the end of our month, we are left with little or no energy to effectively care for ourselves, much less be fully present for our families and those we love. All we want to do is build a legacy for our families with the option to do what we absolutely love day in and day out with time to spare.

To be wealthy, remain wealthy, and free up time on our calendar, we must create multiple streams of income. Moreover, we need to feel connected and committed to those streams in order to push through those less-than-exciting, less-than-inspiring entrepreneurial moments, which is why this book is exclusively devoted to accentuating that passion-based business.

In "GET ON THE 7 STREAMS TEAM: HOW TO DISCOVER YOUR MULTIPLE STREAMS OF INCOME," *you will learn how to launch passive income streams directly related to your already-in-progress, wakes-you-up-at-night, keeps-you-motivated, innovative, problem-solving, love-laced, passion-based business.*

Why You Need This Book

As entrepreneurial innovators, we have amazing ideas; not necessarily wheel-reinventing, super-fresh, brand-spanking-new ideas. But perhaps we have just discovered a few unique ways to solve some common, seemingly unsolvable problems. We then share it with someone close we trust who will provide us with honest feedback sans celebratory or obligatory fillers. They agree. Your idea is ingenious. But wait! You have a plethora of ideas. *That's great!* you both say--but you're scatterbrained and need better focus. There is some truth to that last point but not so much to the first. Do not ascribe to being a scatterbrain at all! Simply recognize that you have a multitude of unique ideas and simply need to funnel them into a streamlined system in order to fulfill them all. Is that crazy? Well, am *I* crazy? Maybe! But that's probably what it takes! You AND I are that unorthodox smart kind of crazy.

. As you read through this book, you'll be reminded of many of the ideas you have had and shelved because they didn't quite fit into what you were convinced was the *norm* at the time. You will, for instance, remember the blog you started a few years back that didn't get off the ground and the tee shirt line you thought would sell but you couldn't find the right printer. As you travel from chapter to chapter, from stream to stream, you will find yourself smoothly flowing from one idea to the next—but this time you have a PLAN.

Truth is, you probably started several things and found yourself only passionate about one. That's perfect, because your passion is where it all truly began and now it truly *begins*. Passion is the waterfall of all other streams—the flow, if you will. If you're passionate about more than one thing, no problem; you are invited to follow the process outlined in this book the same way. It's just not recommended that you pursue both passions, simultaneously. You might find one of them fits snugly underneath or even within the other.

When you "GET ON THE 7 STREAMS TEAM," expect to become a builder, a general contractor, an electrician of vision. You will build your very own personal empire. I designed the blueprint. You complete the construction. You will select "the what" in each stream, and I will show you "the how." Alas, you will flick the switch and shine those bright lights of vigor, enthusiasm and, as my Mom used to say, the "stick-to-it-tiveness" (or "sticktuitiveness") which will give your visions lasting power!

If you're ready, say "I'm ready!"

Note to the impatient, rushaholics, and fellow speed-demons: Getting on the 7 STREAMS TEAM, like life, is a journey—not a race. If you feel the way I used to, you believe you have wasted too much time already, are running out of it, and want to get it all done yesterday. I get it. I have the team tees, matching socks, and ball cap to prove it—but rushing this process will not produce legacy-like results. You will burn out quickly if you do not pace yourself and execute each stream with diligence and excellence. Executing doesn't make each stream more successful; it just makes it fast. Your goal is to be more successful, right? Then take your time. Read—no, *study* this book from beginning to end. Take notes in your "little book of big ideas" as you study. Jot down your ideas. Answer the questions in each chapter. Review your notes and then build.)

Who Has Multiple Streams of Income?

The wealthy. The financially wise. So, what do they know that you and I don't (or didn't)? Nothing spectacular, really—just that diversification is key to mitigating risk. I know. I know. That's a mouth full. The wealthy know and have been taught generation after generation not to put all their eggs in one basket. Like the diversification of stocks, they diversify their efforts by launching or investing in multiple ventures. They don't quit their day jobs because that tends to be the seed money required to pursue those ventures. By the time they quit that day job, they are well on their way to success with six- and seven-figure earning enterprises. This group is less emotional about what they *want* to do and focus primarily on what they *need* to do NOW in order to live the life that will allow them to do whatever they want, wherever they want. They start small and make sure their businesses can be readily duplicated. But for us—the solopreneurs and womenpreneurs—we must be able to duplicate ourselves via delegation and automation, **the Leverage-It! Stream**. They take care to get all legal matters properly handled first before pursuing social media congratulations and popularity. They focus on the tactical and practical THEN move on to the beautiful and the sensational.

It is much easier to build the legs of a company when you have already built a profitable *passion-based* brand.

Why Do You Need Multiple Streams of Income?

To be wealthy. To leave a legacy for your children and your children's children. To feel fulfilled. To do what you love. To make money while you sleep so your picture will hang on mantles for the next century, and you will be regarded as the one who made the sacrifices so they didn't have to.

Who Is This Book NOT For?

It is assumed you are either planning to launch a business in the short term or already have one, and your business plan is complete. It is also assumed you are interested in learning how you can "do it all" and still have a life. If you do not plan to be an entrepreneur, have no interest in business ownership or the highs and lows of creating multiple streams of income, this book is probably not for you. On the contrary, if you are indeed interested in learning the concepts presented in this book for the purpose of personal development, you will probably discover some interesting nuggets herein.

When Do You Start Creating?

Chances are you already have a business in progress. If so, read and study the book from beginning to end before beginning the work on your multiple streams. If you don't, begin planning once you complete this book. Remember: It is important that you get the wide-angle view, the macro view, so that you can see your brand model before construction commences. Just as a city plans to erect a majestic skyscraper, a detailed, well-designed model (landscaping and all) is created to attract the perfect RFPs (Request for Proposals), investors, etc. Business or no business, do not consider development until you reach the end.

Okay. Let's jump in!

Chapter 1:

PASSION FORWARD!

"My mission in life is not merely to survive, but to thrive and to do so with some passion, some compassion, some humor and some style."

– Dr. Maya Angelou

A re you really sure about what you love to do?

It's unfortunate how many of us are unclear about what drives us. We have phenomenal skill sets, have attended (or are attending) the top shelf universities/colleges, and have handsomely paying jobs . . . but are we fulfilled? Are *you* fulfilled? Is what you're doing everything you aspired to do? As Dr. Angelou clearly stated, "My mission in life is not merely to survive, but to thrive . . ." Life is about living and *thriving*, and each of us knows we have to work to eat; so shouldn't the work we do provide us the freedom to live a thriving life?

As you embark upon the journey of building multiple streams of income, setting a foundation with the business you are most passionate about is key. The six streams of income referred to in this writing will be the colorful offspring of your passion. That *passion-based* business will be your "active" *stream*—the one you work on daily—while the others will be "passive." Passive income is like a Crockpot meal. There's some preparation to it but after 'while you can pretty much "set it and forget it." Rather, active income is more like ol' skool cooking—like creamy grits-- you'll need to watch the pot.

If you're clear on what you absolutely love doing and have selected to construct a business on that foundation so you can make a living doing that very thing, continue reading this writing. If you're still undecided, this is the perfect opportunity to do some digging. Cleanse your mind of what others have said you should do or what they thought you would become and return to that innocent place where you first uttered, "I want to do THIS for the rest of my life!"

What exactly *is* passion? I'm glad you asked.

Your *passion* selected you! Your *passion* is often your first love. Whether it was watching your grandmother cook and not being able to wait to learn all that good stuff for yourself or dressing up your Barbie Doll in your latest paper fashion creations or drawing objects in the living room or taking apart every piece of your dad's electronic equipment just to see if you could put it back together. A sensation has been overwhelming you each time you come in contact with that activity. I understand many of you know this to be true and married your passion long ago, but if you have been wondering how to effectively *monetize* it or simply expand your moneymaking opportunities, we will explore this in the following chapters. That passion, that hunger, is your foundational resource for establishing your enterprise—your *passion-based business*.

Well, what WOULD you do if money were no object? Don't second-guess it. The first thing that came to mind is most likely it. Is it what your current business is focused upon or is it something else? If it's something else, you're not alone.

About seven years ago, I was knee deep in the fashion industry. A partner and I had created a unique custom apparel collection for a specific target market, and it was catching on…fast. However, I wasn't necessarily motivated by the idea of fashion as much as I was motivated by the newly found confidence I witnessed in our customers when wearing our clothes. It didn't click immediately, but down the road I realized I wasn't passionate about the fashion industry or clothes or even style. I was passionate about the uplifting, the promotion, and the evolution of women. It took seven years and even longer if I recant the many industries I've tested on my way to unveiling my true *passion*.

SKILL vs. PASSION

What you know how to do best may not be the best thing for you to do. Yet, it may be the very thing you've always wanted to do.

One day, my mother and I were discussing the meaning behind "means to an end." We discovered during our conversation that for many of us, passion is reflective of "the end" versus "the means." See, she worked really hard to provide me with a great life, an excellent education, and meaningful experiences. Her work was something she was extremely skilled at but she was most passionate about the opportunities it afforded me. I was her passion. The journey was one of those "it is what it is and I'm thankful for it" journeys. It wasn't what she dreamt about all night or what she pondered upon waking. Her work, her job, was the vehicle she used to fulfill her passion of being an amazing mom!

About 10 years ago, I met a sought-after corporate attorney named Landa. She had one of those fancy corner offices in the center of downtown and everyone seemed to know her name. I scheduled an appointment to discuss my interest in filing articles of incorporation for a company I was preparing to open. About fifteen minutes into the consultation, I asked her these questions . . .

Do you love the work you do?

She stammered for a second. (I imagine she was a bit caught off guard.)

"I've been doing this for years and it's all I ever wanted to do."

I continued . . . But do you love the work?

"I imagine I do since I continue to do it," she said with a chuckle.

Ten years later, we still keep in touch. Ironically, she quit practicing law about three years after our first meeting. I'm not certain our conversation was her turning point, but Landa now writes legal documents for a living. That's what she enjoyed the most about practicing law. It wasn't litigating and such; it was helping others safeguard themselves and their corporations by providing them with ironclad contracts. That was her passion and it took time, years, a bunch of trial and error, and law school money and student loans to figure it out!

So. . .

Can your skill be your passion?
Absolutely!

Can your skill simply be a gateway to that passion?
Absolutely x2!

Could it be that your skill is "apples and oranges" to your passion?
YUP!

The objective is that you unveil exactly what it is so that you can begin to build a legacy based on doing work you love to do.

PREPARE TO MONETIZE YOUR PASSION

*F*or entrepreneurs and aspiring entrepreneurs alike, the goal is to make a profit doing that awesome thing that drives us. Whether we're creating beaded jewelry, natural skincare products, cupcakes, mobile applications, web design packages, or something else, there are several ways we can begin earning in the short term.

Prepare by identifying . . .

- your unique solution to a common problem;
- who your target audience is or will be;
- the value you versus your customer will place on your offering

Check out **this page** for a growing list of **resources** to assist you in building a lasting brand that makes money!

Now, Ask Yourself . . .	**My Answers**
What is my passion?	
What is my natural gift?	
What is my natural talent?	
What is my greatest skill?	
Do I enjoy the work I'm doing?	
Who's it for?	
What difference does it make?	
Why will folks pay me for it?	
What's my ultimate goal? (i.e., wealth, quick cash flow, leave my job, etc.)	

Download this infographic & join the community of entrepreneurs who is living their passion!

Chapter 2:

NICHE IT!

"If everyone is doing it one way, there's a good chance, you can find your niche by going exactly in the opposite direction."

– Sam Walton

*I*n the previous chapter's ***"Now Ask Yourself"*** (which you will see at the close of each of the following chapters), you were encouraged to share your unique solution to a common problem and who the solution is for. This is critical not only for your own edification, but for your pockets. Knowing this seemingly small amount of information will show you where your profit will come from and where to spend it on marketing.

A **buyer persona** is a semi-fictional representation of your ideal customer based on market research and real data about your existing customers. –Hubspot.com

I cannot begin to tell you how many clients over the years have said, "My *(insert any product or service)* is for everyone." My question has consistently been, "How will you reach 'everyone'?" The fact is "everyone" should not be your ideal customer. (I know that's a little opinionated but unless you're the Walmart or Apple of your industry, serving every demographic and psychographic will pose an overwhelming—and probably an unrealistic—challenge.)

To dig deep into the **Niche It!** stream, you must understand what a niche is and who your ideal target audience is. *So, then . . .*

What is a niche [or niche market]?

A niche market is a portion of a **market** that you've identified as having some special characteristic and one that is worth **marketing** to.

Who is your ideal target audience?

Your ideal target audience includes those you desire to specifically attract and those whose void you are filling. To get their attention, however, you must do more than just launch your website and post social media pages. You must actually target them, and the first way to do so is to *IDENTIFY THE WHO, WHAT, WHERE, WHEN, WHY, AND HOW* of that market. In simpler terms, you need to know their *buyer persona*.

HubSpot.com defines buyer persona as:

> *A semi-fictional representation of your ideal customer based on market research and real data about your existing customers.*

> *When creating your buyer persona(s), consider including customer demographics, behavior patterns, motivations, and goals. The more detailed you are, the better. Buyer*

personas provide tremendous structure and insight for your company.

A detailed buyer persona will help you determine where to focus your time, guide product development, and allow for alignment across the organization. As a result, you will be able to attract the most valuable visitors, leads, and customers to your business.

Entrepreneur.com's 3 rules of niche marketing:

1. **Meet their unique needs.** The benefits you promise must have special appeal to the market niche.

2. **Say the right thing.** When approaching a new market niche, it is imperative to speak their language.

3. **Always test-market.** Before moving ahead, assess the direct competitors you'll find in the new market niche and determine how you will position against them.

After identifying your ideal market, consider multiplying your potential income by segmenting that market into smaller ones. **It is much easier to hit a big mark on a smaller target.** Theoretically, in the end you become the mayor of several tiny towns because frankly, there is less competition.

Take for example my target audience of women entrepreneurs. That is a super broad and competitive market. Purchasing advertising to reach this overly saturated group would be both costly and, as a small business, not nearly as effective as reaching smaller groups within the large one. It is time to segment it or rather, *Niche It!* I will have greater success aiming for one dozen small niches than one large one.

Niche Your Niche

With each niche, your opportunity to become the preferred expert increases. Your marketing angles and strategies become more simplified (because you're not trying to reach everyone). Your promotional efforts will be easier to measure and scale. Your "buyer" will feel like your brand messaging is speaking directly to them. Niching your niche is a personal brand and profit-enhancing strategy from which we can all benefit! Not to mention, you can *re*-niche your market and drill it down smaller and smaller at any time. You control how much money you want to earn.

Now, Ask Yourself . . .   **My Answers**

Who is my niche?

Why them?

How can I become the mayor of several tiny towns?

How will I market to my niche?

What are twelve mini-niches I can identify to grow my company?

Download this infographic & join the entrepreneurs who are becoming the mayors of tiny towns they created!

Chapter 3:

LEVERAGE IT!

"Good people hire people better than themselves. So A players hire A+ players. But others hire below their skills to make themselves look good. So B players hire C players. C players hire D players, etc."

– Guy Kawasaki

When my son was an infant, he was on a pretty tight schedule. Naps, baths, meals; they were each predictable day in and day out. If he ever had medicine to take, both the doses and the times to take them were threaded into his standard schedule. The very moment I needed a babysitter (specifically, Grandma), I wrote it all down so she could follow the schedule and nothing would change for him.

Our businesses can and should work similarly. But if you were to vacation for one whole month, would your business die without you, barely survive, or thrive in your absence?

SOPs: *Standard Operating Procedures*... a set of step-by-step instructions that achieve a predictable, standardized, desired result often within the context of a longer overall process. - Wikipedia

How to Clone Yourself

"I wish I could clone myself," stated by countless individuals who are stretched to their limits. What they desire is not totally unreachable. It's why some folks hire maids, virtual assistants, booking agents, marketing agencies, and even babysitters. They need the help! At some point, they want to do more than be task-masters and have more time while still enjoying their lives.

Entrepreneurs are no different. You need the help and you need to keep the finances flowing! Wouldn't it be divine if you had someone you could leave your "baby" (that is, your business) with and continue serving your customers in your absence? This way you could embrace the sands of Dubai or ocean-hugging St. Croix for a month while your company continued to make money and operate efficiently. This is a desire/goal for many of us, but the thought of delegating is daunting and for those who have been "burned," it's absolutely frightening. But not doing so leaves money on the table and inevitably empties your personal energy reserves.

Delegation seems to be more of an art than a skill—unfortunate but true, simply because good people *are* hard to find. Yet taking the risk to delegate will afford you opportunities to tend to other shelved projects you're passionate about or even better, DO SOMETHING FUN AND RELAXING! Just think of it . . . what if you were able to attend a major conference in your industry, network with those "major players" all while your organization was being tended to (in your signature way)? Or even better, DO SOMETHING FUN AND RELAXING!?!

To prepare you and your business for such expansion, you need to write it all down in the form of standard operating procedures (SOPs), *"a set of step-by-step instructions to achieve a predictable, standardized, desired result often within the context of a longer overall process." (Wikipedia)*

Don't be taken aback by the thought of a 100-page bound book nestled underneath the cash wrap of a brick and mortar store if that's not your setup. Remember that note I left for Grandma with all the instructions for babysitting my son? That was a simple (but very important) form of my "Babysitter SOPs." Of course, Grandma had foundational knowledge rearing children so I didn't include such instructions like how to hold him and keep him safe. It is expected that you would only delegate duties to someone with some foundational knowledge.

Click here to get simple tips for creating an SOP for your small business.

The Joy of Automation

The last time you signed up for someone's email newsletter, did you notice how often you received emails? Whether weekly or monthly, did you think the author wrote each email that day or the day before it was sent to you? The truth is they planned the messages they wanted you to receive in a sequence, scheduled and automated them in their email campaign software like Aweber. This way they guarantee every subscriber receives the same track of emails and they only needed to sit down and pound those emails out once.

Like delegation, automation frees you up to apply yourself to other moneymaking opportunities. Once your business is automated you can tackle new streams of income!

11 Ways to Automate Your Business Today

1. Administration = Hire a Virtual Assistant or Evernote

2. Social Media Marketing = Hootsuite

3. Email = Check email no more than twice a day at the same time each day

4. Email Marketing = Autoresponders

   - Autoresponders are emails that are sent out automatically in a sequence that you determine. (MailChimp, Aweber, Constant Contact, etc.)

5. Blogging = Wordpress Scheduling

6. Receipts = Shoeboxed

7. Web support for your company or website = Zen Desk

8. Teamwork and Project Management = SmartSheet

9. Hiring & Recruitment Software = Recruiter Box

10. Budgeting = Concur

11. Shopping Carts and Online Ordering = Woo Themes

Now, Ask Yourself . . .	My Answers
Can my business live without me?	
How would my life change if I began delegating?	
When will I begin developing my SOPs?	
What processes can I automate right now?	

Download this infographic & join the group of small business owners who are making a living LIVING!

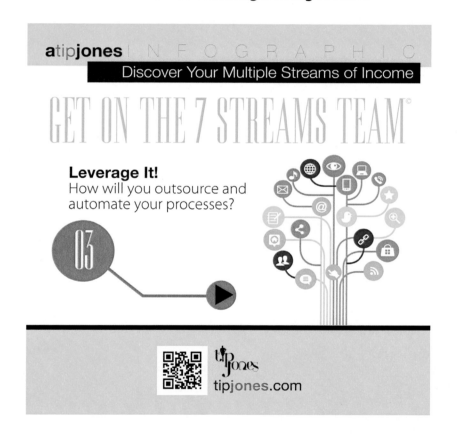

Chapter 4:

TEACH IT!

"If you think in terms of a year, plant a seed; if in terms of ten years, plant trees; if in terms of 100 years, teach the people."

– Confucius

We all have taught someone something at some time in our lives. Whether it was training a new employee at work, tutoring our local youth, or showing someone a dance step, we have been in the role of "teacher."

It may not be your primary gift but you are capable of sharing what you know through blood, sweat, tears, and experience with hungry, attentive listeners. With some structure and planning, you can expand your brand to include coaching, consulting, workshops, webinars, and teleseminars. Allow me to share: While growing up I was a bit anxious about what I wanted to be. Most children already knew by age five—*What do you want to be when you grow up, Betty? Jerry? Pam? Betty: I wanna be a nurse. Jerry: I wanna be a rock star! Pam: I wanna be President of the United States of America!*

Having not a clue of my own, I was truly not in that category until age ten. My Mom told me she thought I'd be a teacher. *Nuh-*

uh! Not I! Said I. At ten, I was certain I wanted to work in medicine as a pediatrician or obstetrician. I was not going to be the one standing before a classroom of misbehaving elementary or you-can't-teach-me-nuthin' junior high or high school children.

Oddly enough, in addition to tutoring and helping others with homework in my afterschool program, I learned I thoroughly enjoyed sharing what I had learned with others, especially dance. From age seven to fifteen, I absorbed quite a bit about all types of dance—from tap and ballet to South African Boot Dance and modern dance. Thus, as my Mom kept me with her always engaged in creative activity in our community, for our afterschool production showcase of various local talent I taught the younger students step dances I created. I was, therefore (*drum roll, please*), TEACHING (and I was being compensated)!

So, although teaching might not be your primary gift, you are certainly capable of sharing what you know of whatever blood, sweat, and tears experience you possess with eager, attentive listeners. Add structure and planning, and you can expand your brand to include coaching, consulting, workshops, webinars, and teleseminars.

Basically, I said all of that to say this: An entrepreneur will indeed teach SOMEbody SOMEthing SOMEwhere at SOME time.

Which of those should you consider? Coach or consult? Workshop, webinar, or teleseminar? I recommend doing a combination of them all—but let us first address the difference between coach and consultant.

John Jantsch of Duct Tape Marketing says

> *To me a coach is charged with holding a client accountable to stated actions, goals and courses while a consultant is more likely to feel empowered to set the course of action.*

*In my mind there probably is no pure definition because a marketing coach or a marketing consultant, for instance, doing the best they can for a customer, will likely fall into a **hybrid** service to get the ball moving forward in any way possible.*

I am confident you are already holding others accountable to be great while introducing them to a "system of achievement." That system (your *signature system*) can easily become an online program on sites like:

Udemy.com

Jigsawbox.com

Teachable.com (*here, you can create your very own academy*)

As an integral part of your system or program, you can begin your sales funnel (*the process by which you transition leads to customers*) with free webinars or teleseminars. This is where you provide a wide-angle view of your selected topic to as many people in your target audience as possible. With your dynamic voice and presentation, no doubt a good percentage of them will be interested in your paid offerings, *e.g.*, online coaching program or modules, live trainings, group coaching, and one-on-one coaching.

For our edification, I paraphrase *Confucius—if you desire a legacy, teach people.*

Now, Ask Yourself . . .	**My Answers**
How many people call me each month asking for my advice?	
Do I prefer virtual or live speaking?	
What type of coaching programs would my target audience benefit from?	
What are ten niches topics you can teach?	
What is preventing me from creating them today?	

Download this infographic & join the host of entrepreneurs who are using workshops, coaching, teleseminars, and webinars to enhance their brands!

Chapter 5:

WRITE IT!

"Either write something worth reading or do something worth writing."

— Benjamin Franklin

Everyone has a story to tell. Like teaching, whether the story is personal or professional, comical or conservative, each of us has a distinctive experience worth sharing. The written word stands alone on its own merit, but add it to the spoken word and you have the potential to truly position yourself as an expert on your *passion-based* topic.

> "Write the vision and make it plain on tablets that he may run who reads it..." - Habukuk 2:2 (NKJV)

On a Friday morning, I was sitting alone in a coffee shop at a table for eight with my MacBook Pro, croissant, notebooks spread about, and large water. I know I looked as if I had been there a while or would be. A woman sat across from me at a much smaller table working on her tablet. Every few moments I could feel her looking over at me.

Finally, she asked: *"What are you working on?"*

"A non-fiction book," I replied with a focused but unintentional 'PLEASE DO NOT DISTURB' look on my face.

> *"That's wonderful! I've been working on a book for a while,"* she shared.
>
> *"When will the world get to read it?,"* I asked nosily.
>
> *"I should be finished with it next week…next month…I don't know. It needs editing but it's poetry and I don't want anyone changing my words and such, you know?"*

Have you wanted to write a book? Have you started one or two or even three titles? Have you written a book but have barely made sales? Have you made excuses about why you have not finished that book you were once so excited about writing? You're not alone but the unfortunate truth is: you're leaving passive income on the table.

I know a book takes time to write, proofread, edit, design, and lay out, but once completed it does not need to be completed again (that is, unless you do a revised version). The next step is to share it with your target audience. With your various niches laid out in the **Niche It!** stream, you now have small groups you can market to. Since you've positioned yourself as a subject matter expert amongst these groups, it will be less difficult to make sales.

So why would anyone delay completing a book that will garner additional income not otherwise tapped into?

Time

Let me remind you of something you have probably read on countless blogs or in books about: *you can write a book in 30 days!* (There are even some schools of thought that suggest you can write it in 15 days.) I'm a bit of a traditionalist, so I still work with keyboards, pens and paper—but you can do like many others and write your book with your voice. If you have a smartphone, chances are there is a voice recorder factory-installed. Now you can "speak your book" and time becomes much less a hindrance to you accomplishing your writing goals.

If you have already successfully written and self-published your book, but have experienced real issues with consistent income, an ironclad marketing plan would do you some good. You can supplant the need for more hours in your week by engaging your **Leverage It!** stream and hiring a publicist or marketer to get you over the hump. Where there's a will, there is always a way!

Affordability

Self-publishing isn't actually costly. It's all the steps that lead up to getting your book on <u>Amazon.com</u> and <u>Createspace. com</u> that prick your affordability nerve.

Once you've written the book, you will need to have it professionally proofread and copy edited. (If you spoke the book, you will need to have it transcribed first and still proofread and edited.) This critical step should never be skipped. Have you read a book, e-book, white paper and found typographical and spelling errors? What was your impression? Exactly! Everything about the content and the author was now in question— albeit, on trial. Proofreading and copyediting will safeguard you from serious reputational risk; so the investment is absolutely worth it.

A sensational book cover designed by a pro graphic artist will set your book apart from many other self-published authors. The cost for this service could be as low as $5 on Fiverr.com or hundreds more dollars by a local graphic artist in your city. Nevertheless, it's a one-time cost.

There are other expenses you can incur like booking a professional photo shoot for your author headshot, having a 3D version of your book designed for sharing on social media and your blog, and more. But the bare bones of your expenses are cover design and proofreading/copy editing.

Support (or lack thereof)

Now to the nitty-gritty. It's terribly difficult to write when those around you won't provide you with the space to be creative; or if you live alone, those who care for you don't encourage you to get it done. This is one of the many times you must encourage yourself. Your book, whether a fictional tale filled with imaginary characters or your personal memoirs or a how-to book, has the potential to open eyes and minds. Your perspective is unique, and there are many of us who are waiting for someone to "spell it out" for us in a way only you can. So, if no one has told you that *you can* or *I believe in you*, I'm telling you right now: *You can. You should. I believe in you!*

Your book is more than a stream of income, frankly. It is a **legacy-building** tool even if it never makes a dime. You instantly become a published author. It's an accomplishment and since you're still reading, I get the impression it's one you are aiming to reach.

Tip Jones

Other Ways to Write It!

- Freelance writing – magazine articles, ghost-writing
- Create free content for download to promote paid content
- Turn one big book idea into 3-5 small book ideas (people want/need small, digestible pieces)
- And of course, blogging – guest blogging and hosting your own blog

Now, Ask Yourself . . .	My Answers
What's my story?	
What topics will I be teaching? Can I write about them, too?	
Do I prefer to go 'ol skool and type or use my voice recorder?	
Who will hold me accountable for completing my book?	
How can I break down my big book idea into a series of smaller books?	
What's preventing me from earning money by writing about what I know?	

Download this infographic & join entrepreneurs who are using blogs and books to become experts in their industries!

Chapter 6:

NETWORK MARKET IT!

"...I believe that the entire industry is poised for explosive growth and can be one of the most significant solutions to America's current retirement savings crisis."

– Robert Laura, Forbes.com

etwork marketing is a controversial topic for several people. Experience with scams and schemes have made some of the smartest people, at the very least, apprehensive—and others downright afraid—to ascribe to the fee structures or listen to the hype testimonials of those who have already risen to the top. Similar to other areas in life, one rotten apple can indeed spoil the whole bunch.

Network marketing is a viable stream of income for hundreds of thousands of people. It's an inexpensive way to buy into a business (like you would a franchise) without investing in production costs, customer service agents, advertising, etc. The products and the marketing plans are already created for you. You need only share it with others. Interestingly enough, we will share our experience of the latest restaurant—the tasty dishes, price point, and even how to get there—but too many of us shudder at the idea of sharing the business we are in. Why? Because it just *feels* like selling.

The truth is, once you *stop selling* and *stop thinking you are selling*, you will realize what you are actually doing is presenting someone with an opportunity. That opportunity could be better skin using Avon products, more opportunities to travel and have fun using DreamTrips, on-call legal assistance through PrePaid Legal or sustainable weight loss and greater health with HerbaLife. This same opportunity also provides a chance to earn a referral bonus, commission and, ultimately, a salary. *You're not selling a product—you're sharing a lifestyle benefit.*

Why are so many entrepreneurs not tapping into this tried-and-tested passive stream of income? Frankly, too often the presentation sucks! Some way-too-excited individual stands before a roomful of folks and says,

> *"Write down the names of all your friends and family, call each one of them and tell them what you're doing and that you want them to buy from you or help you sell and join your team."*

Whoa! Whoa! Whoa! Pipe down. Most of us have attended this meeting, and it's pretty doggone scary. All of a sudden it feels like if we don't bring our entire Rolodex of friends and contact all of our family members, success is not in our future. This model has worked for some but not most.

How to Make Network Marketing Work For You... Your Way

The network marketing company you consider must be closely related to your *passion-based business*. It should provide a service or product *your* clientele will spend money on after working with you. This is critical.

For instance, makeup artists may not all be estheticians, but their clients trust them with their skin. They are asked about best skincare practices, best cleansers and moisturizers to use before and after the application of makeup. They have an opportunity to profit from their referrals without appearing "salesy." If the make-up artist (MUA) is an independent distributor of Mary Kay, s/he has the opportunity to share cleansing cloths, astringents, and facial lotions, thus making themselves increasingly more valuable to their clients.

Providing value, improving someone's situation, or changing someone's life—or even one's outlook on life—motivates many of us to work harder each day on our enterprises. We meet incredible people, like-minded people, and build wealth while bringing others with us. The foundation is set. The blueprint is there. We need only follow it and expose someone else to it who we believe deserves to hear about it.

The NO FRILLS Truth About Network Marketing

Despite what folks have tried to convince us network marketing is, its success does not happen overnight. It's not for getting rich quickly. It's a trustworthy tool for building wealth, methodically. Three to five years consistently "pressing play" in the organization of your choice has the potential to provide you with residual income for many years.

Sweat equity will be your largest initial investment in any passive income stream. Consider this book I've written. It took time to write, rewrite, have proofread, copyedited, graphically designed, optimized for the device you're reading it on, published, and marketed. Eventually, I will move on to writing other books as this one exists on the World Wide Web, available for purchase without my constant involvement.

Take a second look at network marketing. (If this is your first time being introduced to it, then I am honored.)

What services or products do your clients purchase after working with you?

What have you wanted to sell but don't have any interest in creating from scratch?

How have you wanted to further enhance your life and what company do you believe can assist you in attaining that goal?

My answer was twofold: I desperately wanted to travel while I worked but had no clue how I could do so on a reasonable budget. I also had no leisure outlets and had a hard time figuring out what I wanted to do for fun—then I became ill. The doctor thought I was having a heart attack (because I had all the symptoms except one); however, the EKG was normal. So what on earth was wrong here? As it turns out, it was stress. The doctor asked me very gently, "What do you do for fun?" I said honestly, "I work on my projects, my business. They're my first loves." Then he made a crystal clear point. He sat down on the little black stool in the examination room and said, "Your brain does not differentiate between work and work. It differentiates between rest and work. So although you love what you're doing, you need to fall in love with something that simply satisfies the pleasure centers of your brain."

It took me 48 hours to figure out what I enjoyed doing for fun. I LOVE TO TRAVEL. I had only thought about traveling as it pertained to visiting clients, hosting workshops, and covering events in other cities and countries. I had forgotten how much I loved doing it just for fun. It was around this same time my very good friends introduced me to <u>World Ventures</u>. Now, as they say, "I can make a living LIVING."

Click <u>here</u> for the best multi-level marketing companies of 2015.

See what network marketing company **ranks** the best <u>here</u>.

> *"Network marketing gives people the opportunity with very low risk and very low financial commitment to build their own income generating asset and acquire great wealth."*

> **– Robert Kiyosaki**

Now, Ask Yourself . . .   **My Answers**

What services do my customers use after working with me?

How can I benefit from being a part of a much larger group of like-minded individuals?

What company will I select as my 6th passive stream of income?

Download this infographic & join other network market-preneurs successfully diversifying their income!

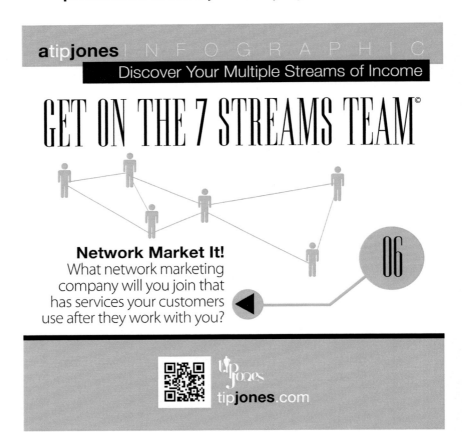

Chapter 7:

SELL IT!

"Create something, sell it, make it better, sell it some more and then create something that obsoletes what you used to make."

– Guy Kawasaki

Although we have covered quite a bit of ground up to this point, there is still more worth exploring to earn you more passive income.

You are now all set to sell those books you're writing, promote your teaching events, sell your online coaching programs, and still there are several other ways you can make additional passive income from your *passion-based business*.

A few months ago, I was speaking with Lisa, an aspiring photographer. She had been in the modeling industry for twenty years, the wardrobe styling industry for more than fifteen years, and producing photo shoots for three. It seemed to be the natural order of things to fire the middleman and become the photographer she always relied upon and desired to be. While courting various online and offline programs, she began looking into office space and studio space to host her shoots. Studio rent in her city was, as we sometimes say, "nothing to sneeze at!" For a moderately sized square space it was double the cost of her residential rent in the suburbs. Immediately, she began pondering whether this was going to be a wise venture. So, she asked herself three desperate questions . . .

> - ➢ *"What if I have an entire month with no clients?"*
> - ➢ *"What about the cost of electricity, Internet, and water?"*
> - ➢ *"What about parking? OMGoodness! What if I have to pay for parking?"*

Apprehensive and afraid, she was attempting to cover all of her bases. As her business coach, I was ecstatic! Because for each potential problem there is an attainable solution, and I love a good "mystery" worth solving. What Lisa had on her side was a laundry list of celebrity clientele, a stellar reputation, and the personality to attract her ideal client. All she needed was to figure out how to avoid going broke once she adds the photography stream to her repertoire. Well okay then, let's take a closer look . . .

When her studio space was not in use, Lisa could rent it out to other photographers and stylists (and she knew several of each). Doing so would deliver additional income she didn't need to work very hard for (*passive income*). She would need to actively market the space to those groups (e.g., FREELANCE PHOTOGRAPHERS AND STYLISTS WITHOUT THEIR OWN STUDIO SPACE) at first, and once word-of-mouth took the wheel, she would be able to reduce her investment in advertising, etc. During her slow seasons or slow days, Lisa could also rent out the space as <u>coworking space</u>, where individuals get to collaborate or just share entrepreneurial energy that is simply unavailable at their home offices.

Now, let that marinate a little bit. You see where this is going?

Do you have a brick and mortar store, loft, or space? Consider ways you can share the space with colleagues and other entrepreneurs in your area. Hmm?

Sell Space on Your (very reputable) Website

In this day and age, every business must have a website. It's what the consumer expects; and if they can't find you in the palm of their hands, you won't be found or worse, sought out.

Now that that's out of the way, let's take a look at your blog, your minisite for your books or your website. The sidebar on it and the space above-the-fold is prime real estate for Google AdSense advertisements and personally sold ads. If you have a considerable amount of monthly traffic on your website, do not pass up the opportunity to acquire additional revenue by selling ad space.

Get Paid for Your Referrals Immediately!

I have always appreciated the generous sharing of experiences, web links, products, restaurants, best places to shop, and such, but where possible and fair, I think one should be compensated for at least half of those referrals (where available, of course). Thankfully, many of the places you support and endorse have established referral programs with comparably generous compensation plans. Be sure to scroll down to the footer of your most visited and most trusted websites to check if they have a resellers or referral program. This is additional income you don't have to do anything extra for. You need only place the appropriate banners or links on your website or in your blog posts and continue driving traffic as you normally would.

Gentle Warning!

I do not suggest that you set your expectations to earning a hefty five hundred dollars in your first month of selling ad space or joining affiliate programs.

The goal is to position yourself to generate income from multiple places that do not require "white glove service."

Ever Considered Franchising?

This one's a biggie! I won't go into detail about the wonderful world of franchising, but once your business is easily duplicable (and you are interested in the process), I strongly encourage you to look into it.

Now, Ask Yourself . . .	**My Answers**
What products can I sell?	
What affiliate programs are best suited for me to join?	
What's my monthly web traffic?	
How can I benefit from Google Adsense or direct-selling ads?	
What are the best times of the month for me to rent my space and to whom?	

**Download this infographic & share it with entrepreneurs
who are maximizing their earning potential!**

DOWNLOAD YOUR FREE INFOGRAPHIC & SHARE IT!

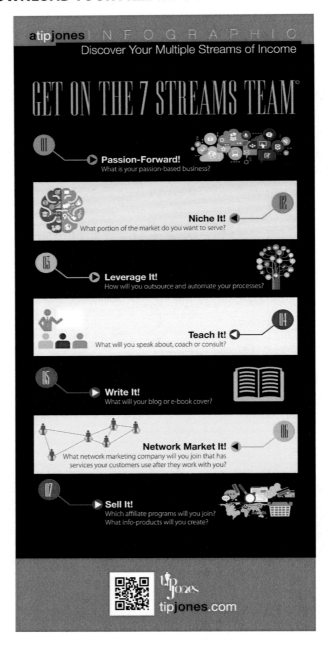

Business Operations Resources for Entrepreneurs

GoDaddy.com – The world's largest technology provider dedicated to small businesses. Domains, web hosting, servers, site builders, custom email, etc.

1and1.com – Domains, web hosting, website builder, eShop and more!

Shoeboxed.com – Shoeboxed is the fast, painless way to digitize and archive receipts in a single, secure location. They turn receipts into extracted, human-verified data that is categorized, organized, fully searchable and available anytime, anywhere.

Dropbox.com – The free service that lets you bring your photos, docs, and videos anywhere and share them easily. Never email yourself a file again! We use Dropbox to store all of our important files, especially the baby and family pics!

Canva.com – Design presentations, social media graphics, and more with thousands of beautiful layouts. We use Canva for various promotions, flyers, and announcements.

Fiverr.com – The global online marketplace offering tasks and services, beginning at a cost of $5 per job performed, from which it gets its name. The site is primarily used by freelancers who use Fiverr to offer services to customers worldwide. Currently, Fiverr lists more than three million services on the site that range between $5 and $500.

SurveyMonkey.com – It's easier than ever to create polls and survey questionnaires for learning about anything from customer satisfaction to employee engagement.

The Coaches Console — Complete online system for managing your entire coaching business. With the Coaches Console you can attract new clients, manage current clients, track client progress, handle call notes, manage billing, email prospects and clients, do online scheduling and much more. Coaches Console is the one place you can come to manage your whole business, so you can focus on coaching clients.

Jigsaw Box — This super easy-to-use online content manager helps you create coaching packages, coursework and templates for your coaching business. Manage your clients and content within one portal and even do "online coaching."

iWriter.com – If you're tired of writing your own content for your website, or just can't find the time to do it yourself, iWriter is the perfect place for you. iWriter is the world's first and only service created solely to facilitate the process of hiring someone to write articles for you, at a price that simply cannot be beat.

Shopping Cart Solutions for Entrepreneurs

Direct Pay – Here's where you can get a Merchant Account so you can accept credit cards and debit cards. They offer competitive rates and work with a lot of women entrepreneurs.

Ontraport — This is an all-in-one business and marketing platform designed for information marketers, experts, and women entrepreneurs. It integrates your contact management, payment processing, automated marketing, task management and affiliate management.

Newsletter & Email List Management Resource for Entrepreneurs

MailChimp — Completely free service for lists up to 2,000 subscribers! We've been using Mailchimp for 5 years and love its easy of functionality.

Aweber – Opt-In email marketing service.

Free and Paid Conference Services

Easy Seminar — This is a robust paid conference call service for conducting professional quality teleseminars and webinars that attract prospects and makes it easy for them to take the "next step" with you. This service provides instant teleseminar or webinar replay and makes it easy for people to participate by phone (with local access numbers in the USA, Canada, Australia and the UK), Skype or webcast.

Maestro Conference — Your webinars and teleconferences can be social, engaging, and interactive. Energize your events with visual screensharing and the intimacy and power of breakout groups. Replicate a live room experience with raised hands, instant polls and more. Social Conferencing gives you the ease and reach of teleconferencing, with the depth of social interactions, in real-time conversations – for a fraction of the cost, time, and hassle of a live meeting.

Free Conference Call — Free conference calls are simple and easy to use, requiring only a name and an e-mail address to receive an instant account. Your teleconferencing line is available to you 24/7 and there is no need to schedule or make reservations. Each conference call account accommodates 96 callers on an unlimited number of 6 hour free conference calls.

Instant Conference — The web-based moderator controls provide your conference organizer with the ability to monitor attendance, and activate call features such as recording or changing the call's muting configuration. An online Control Panel displays available Caller ID information, and you can "ping" individual participants to take roll call.

Free Conference — Web-based conference call scheduling and management tools, as well as conference bridges, are offered entirely free of charge! There is absolutely no catch. This is not a limited-time offer – no gimmicks, no gotchas and no tricks. These standard services are full-featured, with only minimal service limitations. We use Free Conference and love it!

How Entrepreneurs Get Published

BlogTalkRadio.com – Easily Create a Professional Podcast & Reach Millions Today! Get Started with BlogTalkRadio, FREE for 30 Days! BlogTalkRadio is the leading provider of interactive audio technology solutions. They make it easy for anyone, anywhere to produce high-quality broadcasts and share them online. All you need is a phone and a computer to get started.

Createspace.com – You can sell books, CDs, and DVDs for a fraction of the cost of traditional manufacturing, while maintaining more control over your materials. They make it simple to distribute your books, music, and video through Internet retail outlets, your own website, and other bookstores, retailers, libraries, and academic institutions.

LuluJr.com – This is a great self-publishing service that allows children to become published authors, encouraging creativity, strengthening literacy and building self-esteem.

Automation Resources

http://www.mynewcompany.com/automate.htm

http://www.johnchow.com/10-tips-to-automate-your-business/

http://www.digitalmarketer.com/business-automation-tools-email/

Note: The Consulting Studio may have an affiliate relationship with the companies listed above. All this means is that if you decide to invest in one of the resources we recommend, we may receive some type of compensation. We only affiliate with companies that we know can be of great value to you; however, we do recommend that you perform due diligence and <u>use your own judgment when making decisions and investments in your business</u>.

Put this content into practice with the
GET ON THE 7 STREAMS ONLINE COACHING PROGRAM

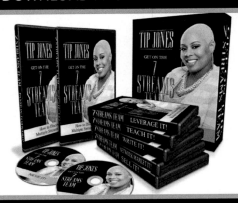
Do you have a ton of ideas you know have excellent potential but you have trouble structuring them?

Are you busy building a legacy for your family while managing every day responsibilities?

Do you work a 9 to 5 but are ready to transition out of it?

Do you envision passing on knowledge, opportunities, but especially financial wealth and wisdom to the next generation?

If you answered YES to any of these questions, this online coaching course is for you!

The "Get on the 7 Streams Team" Online Coaching Course is a *7-Module eCourse to Develop & Construct Your Multiple Streams of Income*

Module 1	PASSION-FORWARD!
Module 2	NICHE IT!
Module 3	LEVERAGE IT!
Module 4	TEACH IT!
Module 5	WRITE IT!
Module 6	NETWORK MARKET IT!
Module 7	SELL IT!

- 7 <u>self-paced</u> modules with more than 100 workbook-style questions.

- Each module will be emailed directly to you after completion of the previous one.

- All 7 modules have been broken down into small, digestible nuggets to help you develop your new streams of income or improve your current ones.

- Each module will take you through a deep dive into each stream to increase your business idea's feasibility and profitability.

- You will learn both the "what to do" and the "how to do" of each stream.

- You will have an opportunity to interact with me directly to ask questions and gain feedback as you go through the program.

- And there's so much more.

START BUILDING YOUR PASSIVE STREAMS OF INCOME TODAY!

Free Access to Module 1: Passion-Forward of the Get on the 7 Streams Team Online Coaching Program

ABOUT THE AUTHOR

Tip Jones is a serial entrepreneur, business coach, and speaker. She has been creating fresh ideas for businesses since age 13. She created and published the award-winning plus size lifestyle publication, *POSE Magazine* and has coached women entrepreneurs since 2007 through her company, The Consulting Studio.

Tip came across countless women-owned small businesses on shoestring budgets with uncontainable passion for their crafts and often very little marketing experience. As the creator of multiple businesses in her teen years and early twenties and predominantly beginning with no money, she found creative ways to get the word out about her businesses. These experiences fueled her desire to teach other "womenpreneurs" how to increase their clientele and customer bases. Within her first year, Tip had twenty dedicated clients whom she consulted on the topics of brand development, web presence, and guerrilla marketing tactics.

Since the early days of exclusively providing consultations, Tip has matured *The Consulting Studio* to the premier destination for women-owned startups and successful solo womenpreneurs who seek coaching, brand development, business-boosting workshops, classes, seminars and more.

In 2015, Tip founded *Confidence University: How to Succeed at Anything!*, a live intensive workshop aimed at enhancing self-esteem while reigniting the innocent fearlessness that allows us all to believe "we can."

UPCOMING TITLES FROM TIP JONES

Get on the 7 Streams Team for Womenpreneurs:
How to Discover Your Multiple Streams of Income

Top 10 Habits of Successful Womenpreneurs:
Redesign Your Life Today

Unstoppable Womenpreneurs:
Affirmations to Grow Your Confidence in 21 Days

Wrap It Up:
Your Shortest Guide to Finishing What You've Started

Broke & Broken:
Your Shortest Guide to Quitting Habits that Break You Down

Made in the USA
San Bernardino, CA
24 August 2016